LEAD OUT

A Guide for Leading Bible Discussion Groups

NAVPRESS
A MINISTRY OF THE NAVIGATORS

Post Office Box 20, Colorado Springs, Colorado 80901

© 1974 by The Navigators
All rights reserved including translation.

ISBN 0-89109-125-4
Fifth Printing, 1978

The Navigators is an international,
interdenominational Christian organization.
Jesus Christ gave His followers
a Great Commission in Matthew 28:19,
"Go therefore and make disciples
of all nations . . ." The primary aim
of the Navigators is to help fulfill
that commission by making
disciples and developing disciplemakers
in every nation

Printed in the United States of America

TABLE
OF
CONTENTS

UNIT ONE
Preparing to Lead a Discussion

UNIT TWO
Improving Your Technique

Preparing to Lead a Discussion

Your Potential as a Discussion Group Leader

The Value of the Discussion Group

Throughout the world today many committed Christians are witnessing the dynamic impact of small Bible discussion groups. Sparked by the growing hunger for personal knowledge of God's Word, these bands of eager learners are springing up everywhere. The intense fellowship, the personal interaction over God's Word and the mutual commitment to application which is experienced in these groups is often unparalleled by other methods of spiritual development. Sometimes the vitality of Christian experience achieved becomes the springboard for a whole new spiritual awakening.

The idea of small groups is not really new. Almost 2,000 years ago, the followers of Jesus Christ met together in homes to study the Word, pray, fellowship together and seek greater outreach in the community. The Book of Acts records the impact of these groups and their experiences in carrying out the Great Commission.

One person with a genuine desire and hunger for the Lord is enough to spark a group. One group, in turn, is enough to ignite a dormitory, military barracks, business office or neighborhood. Motivated men and women in dormitories, barracks, offices, neighborhoods and churches can penetrate and saturate a community with Christ-centered disciples. You could be the person to start this process.

Goal of the Discussion Group

The type of discussion group presented in this booklet is one which assumes prior personal preparation by each participant. Otherwise, the discussions become a substitute for personal study and the time is spent with everyone "sharing their ignorance." Those who have prepared will not learn anything new and, as a result, will soon lose their motivation for personal study. A group discussion among unprepared people will not provide the prayerful meditation and personal confrontation with God's Word that is achieved through personal preparation.

The goal of the discussion group, therefore, is to amplify the results of personal Bible study through the interaction of a small group of people. A successful discussion group:

- Provides an incentive for people to complete their personal Bible study on a regular basis.

- Enables people to go beyond the limits of their own personal findings by exposing them to the ideas of others and by stimulating further thoughts about the material studied.

- Creates an atmosphere which is conducive to honest sharing of personal discoveries, questions, problems or needs. An atmosphere of love and acceptance builds confidence and allows freedom to speak about the Bible without fear of embarrassment or criticism.

- Fosters positive Christian fellowship where group members can develop solid personal relationships in an informal setting. It is here that group members learn how to pray, share and bear the burdens of others.

- Equips young growing Christians with a method of helping others grow spiritually. Bible discussion groups are one of the most effective and simple tools available to Christians today as they seek to help fulfill Christ's Commission to make disciples in every nation.

The Nature of the Discussion Group

Group discussions are not lectures in which an infallible expert displays his knowledge to a captive audience. The lecture has a place in teaching but not in a discussion. It is unnecessary because the members have prepared their studies in advance and are able to share what they have learned.

Group discussions are not conversations where overly opinionated people carry on a dialogue. The quieter members of the group will soon lose interest and may stop coming altogether if they are not given opportunities to share. The spontaneous interaction of a good discussion provides a setting for sharing, learning and making new discoveries.

God's Word achieves its life-changing effect on people through the ministry of the Holy Spirit. The effective discussion leader will act as a chairman and guide, not as a teacher or authority, because he realizes the authority is the Word of God and the teacher is the Holy Spirit. The Scriptures are the sword of the Spirit. The leader's role is to guide the discussion encouraging personal interaction with Scripture and allowing the Holy Spirit to make application according to each individual's need. This means the Bible will be the focus of attention, not the leader.

What ingredients make a group successful? Here's a sure-fire recipe:

- Start with the Word of God and one other person who longs to know God better.
- Sift in a few other learners.
- Blend in a balanced, interesting course of study like the Navigator *Design for Discipleship* series.
- Add a cup of preparation and saturate with prayer.
- Stir in a tablespoon of common sense.
- Drop in a pinch of humor.
- Skim off the "religious twang," the "do's" and "don'ts," and overemotionalism.
- Season with generous portions of acceptance, genuine personal interest and love.

9

- Remove "preachiness," "self-effort" and the "holier-than-thou" attitude.
- Allow the leavening influence of the Holy Spirit to lift hearts to worshipping the Lord Jesus Christ.

Follow this recipe of leading group discussions and they will never burn, overbake, sour or fall flat!

This booklet covers the fundamentals of leading a discussion group. If you are planning to start a group for the first time, it will provide you with a step-by-step explanation of how to draw a group together and prepare yourself to lead the discussion.

If you are looking for some new tips to improve a discussion you are already leading, this material will provide a resource of ideas and practical suggestions as well as a thorough review of basic principles.

The examples throughout this book are from Book 1, "Your Life in Christ," of the Navigator *Design for Discipleship* series.

Organizing a Discussion Group

Attracting People to the Group

Every successful spiritual endeavor begins with prayer. As Jesus saw the spiritual needs of the masses He said, "The harvest is plentiful, but the laborers are few; *pray* therefore the Lord of the harvest to send out laborers into His harvest" (Matthew 9:37,38).

Begin praying daily that God would help you get a discussion group started. Ask God to attract the people He desires to the study, to unify them and to enable you to lead and encourage the group.

Before you start inviting people to a discussion group, determine what type of Bible study you want to do. There are many good materials available for any type of Bible study. Some Navigator materials that may be helpful to you are:

- *Leader's Guide for Evangelistic Bible Studies (Using the Gospel of John).* The leader is the only one who needs to prepare for this type of study.

- *Design for Discipleship.* This series of six booklets helps a Christian grow as a disciple of Jesus Christ.

- *Search the Scriptures.* A method of studying books of the Bible one chapter at a time is presented.

Once you obtain the materials you need, begin inviting people to the study. Whom you invite depends upon what type of study you are planning. For example, you would invite non-Christians to an evangelistic study.

When inviting people be specific. Tell them what you are planning to do, when you plan to meet and how many weeks it will take to complete the course of study. It is a good rule to have the first study course last no longer than six weeks. Then you can make plans with the group for further study. One way to get a neighborhood Bible discussion group started is to invite several people to your home for coffee and dessert. Then you can share your desire to start a Bible discussion group and ask them to join you.

In a dormitory or barracks just invite people to the first session. If you hold it in your room, be sure you have the cooperation of your roommate. Otherwise meet elsewhere – perhaps in a conference room.

At work you may find a few people interested in joining you for discussion during the lunch hour. If you do, remember that you will only have approximately an half-hour. Keep the weekly assignments short so they can be discussed adequately in the time available.

Some do's and don'ts of inviting people

Do:	Don't:
Invite people who have some common interests. It contributes toward better understanding and communication.	Pressure people – eager people are the best students.
Invite people who are roughly your age.	Have more than you can handle – six is probably the maximum number to start with.
Be positive, optimistic and enthusiastic about the study.	Be discouraged if only one person is willing to meet with you. God is intensely interested in the individual.
Ask people to commit themselves to come each week for the specified course and to do the necessary preparation.	

People often accept an invitation to a Bible study and then fail to come. It is easy for them to forget something that is not part of their normal routine. The devil desires to keep people from God's Word and will set obstacles and distractions in the way. Remind them of the study a day or two in advance. After the first couple of weeks this shouldn't be necessary. By then they will have discovered the profit of their Bible discussion group.

Practical Details

Many practical details affect the success of a Bible discussion group. An uncomfortably warm or cold room, kids or pets running around, or studies that run too long can all distract the group members. There are some things which you as the group leader can plan for in advance. You will want to:

Meet in a comfortable atmosphere. The warmness of a living room, the unity of a kitchen table, or the informality of a dorm

12

room or barracks all lend themselves to a learning atmosphere. Your attitude and approach can make the time together friendly, natural and conducive to honest searching.

Make appropriate physical arrangements. Meet in a circle because this is the best arrangement to see and discuss with one another. Plan your seating in advance. Don't sink into a soft chair – be as high or higher than your group for good eye contact.

Maintain good lighting. Lighting will not only help illuminate the room, it also creates a warm feeling. No one should have to look into the sun or toward a bright window.

Provide proper ventilation. Too much heat or cold will make group members uncomfortable. Start with a well-aired room which is warm enough to be comfortable.

Guard against distractions. Pets, TV's, radios, etc. These take attention away from the discussion. Make arrangements with babysitters if they are needed.

You will discover other practical details as you lead your group. Strive for the best possible situation. However, remember God working in hearts is the key to successful Bible study.

Getting the Group Started

It is almost impossible to overestimate the importance of the first meeting. The impressions created during this meeting may influence the participation of the members for weeks to come.

Remember this is a group discussion. You are the leader, not the director. Be unpretentious and honest. Don't assume airs of superiority but exhibit the quiet confidence that comes from having a plan and knowing how to execute it.

Your major objective in this meeting is to get the participants started studying God's Word. There are three major steps to accomplishing this.

Get acquainted with one another so honest discussion and interaction can take place. As each person arrives, introduce him to the others. To help the people remember each other's names call each person by name as often as possible. Name tags can also be useful.

Help them get to know one another by having each person share about himself. Start with general impersonal questions. Home town, occupation and hobbies are good topics to begin with. You should share first. This helps establish what to cover and how long to take.

Asking unusual and unimportant questions can add some humor and help everyone relax. Instead of having everyone answer the same question, you might make cards with different questions and have everyone draw one to answer. Here are some examples to get you started.

"Who was your first girlfriend (boyfriend)?
Tell something about her."

"Who was your fourth grade teacher?
Tell something about her."

"What qualities do you like best in a cookie?"

"What do you like to do best on a rainy day?"

When the group is comprised of Christians you can have each share their testimony next. By this time everyone should feel relaxed in the group.

Explain how the Bible is going to be studied and how it will be discussed in the group. Before you actually begin your explana-

14

tion, pause for prayer. Ask God to guide the discussion and to teach you from His Word.

It is also important that everyone adheres to a set of standards for the study. You, as a leader, should *suggest* these standards. Be sure not to assume a dictatorial attitude and start telling everyone what is expected. Instead you might say something like, "Can we agree that everyone will finish the study before the discussion each week?" (or "complete the assigned lesson?") Everyone should concur on the importance of *attendance* at the discussions and the *preparation* of the Bible study.

Now it is time to introduce the group to the Bible study plan and give them any materials they will need. If you are using printed materials, be sure to go over the introduction and instructions carefully. To help everyone pay close attention, go around the circle having each person read a paragraph. Stop and discuss what has been read whenever a question arises.

Get the people started doing the study. There should be a sense of expectancy in the group. Enthusiasm can often be developed as the people actually do a little of the study. Without leaving their seats, ask them to quietly start working on the first part of their study. This should probably take five to ten minutes.

Then ask the group to share what they have discovered from this little glimpse into God's Word. There probably won't be time to discuss these observations. Instead, work at creating curiosity and anticipation for the rest of the study. For example, you might say:

"I wonder if we will discover a relationship between these things as we complete our study."

"There isn't time to discuss it now, but do you think ... "

"That is an excellent observation. I have a hunch we will see more about that as we complete the study."

Be sure not to disparage the responses from the group at this first meeting ... especially as they share what they learned from the Bible study time. Instead, work at giving sincere compliments. People are encouraged by praise.

As you complete the time of sharing, close in prayer. If you have budgeted your time carefully, you should not be running late. Each of the three steps should take about one-third of your time.

As you adjourn, remind everyone of the time and place of the next meeting and their assignment.

Determining the Objective

Objectives

A good discussion group leader begins with an objective clearly in mind. "He who aims at nothing, hits it every time." So be sure you have an objective in mind. Don't fall into the trap of "flying by the seat of your pants," hoping that everything will work out.

An objective is a brief statement which summarizes what the group should understand and apply by the end of the discussion period. It needs to be stated clearly in one or two short sentences.

A clear objective will help you do three things:

- It will tell you where you are heading with the discussion and give you direction for your questions.

- It will help you evaluate progress at any point during the discussion. After this evaluation, you can make needed adjustments.

- It will allow you to make decisions along the way as to what to discuss. If a tangent issue arises, you can direct the group back to the main goal and temporarily table the tangent.

Before writing an objective, however, you will need to determine an outline for the chapter.

Outlines

The outline is the basic framework which underlies a particular passage or topical study. It consists of a few subpoints which logically break down the chapter into smaller sections. Like a

16

builder looking at the blueprint for a building, you can look at an outline to see the basic framework of the chapter.

In leading a discussion group, an outline will:

- Provide a general direction for the study.
- Help you prepare discussion questions.
- Help you evaluate the progress of the discussion.
- Serve as a teaching aid by helping the group members remember the content of the discussion.

When leading a discussion in the *Design for Discipleship* series, you will find that the outline is already provided for you. It consists of the subtopics that appear in each chapter. For example, the outline for "God Loves You" (Book 1, Chapter 1) is:

    I. "God Created You"
   II. "God Knows You"
  III. "God Loves You"
  IV. "God Made You Part of His Family"

Writing an Objective

The outline provides stepping stones for determining the objective for the discussion. The objective should seek to capture the movement of the outline and bring it to a conclusion. Before writing down the objective, look closely at the chapter subtitles, then write a discussion objective that will insure comprehension of these main points.

Possible objectives for the chapter "God Cares for You" are "For each of the discussion group members to acknowledge God's love by some expression of assurance of salvation" or "For each of the members to express thankfulness for God's love."

Often the chapter title itself will be explicit enough to help you determine the discussion objective. "God Cares for You" indicates the chapter will cover God's love.

It is also important to think of ways you might evaluate whether your objective has been accomplished. In the chapter on God's love, how can you evaluate whether the group understood and applied the truth of God's love? A prayer of thankfulness for God's love, a brief testimony concerning salvation or a new excitement over a verse on assurance would be valid indicators.

Arriving at a group objective and an outline aids the group in the process of discovery. Knowing where you are going and having a basic map of how to get there gives you an advantage in preparing for a group discussion.

The Value of Questions

A good leader helps the members of the group discover biblical truths for themselves. Therefore, it is necessary for discussion group leaders to cultivate the ability to develop and ask the right questions. These questions become the springboard for discussion in the group. He does not simply repeat the questions in the lesson, but formulates questions which will help the members make new discoveries about what they've studied.

Questions are valuable because:

- They help evaluate the group member's understanding, knowledge and progress in learning.
- They cause the group members to think.
- They reflect a personal approach which elicits a personal response.
- They prevent the group leader from becoming the authority figure.
- They allow the group members to discover truth for themselves.

"You start a question and it's like starting a stone. You sit quietly on the top of the hill; and away the stone goes, starting others."

Robert Louis Stevenson

Each member of the group will have completed his study before coming to the discussion group. While preparing his study, he will have applied four essentials of Bible study – observation, interpretation, correlation and application. Understanding these essentials will help you form good discussion questions.

Observation is the act of seeing; taking notice of things as they really are; the art of awareness or giving full attention to what is seen. When studying the Bible it is especially important that observations are accurate; that is, that all observations refer to known or stated facts and are not assumptions based on the known facts.

Interpretation is the step of determining what the author meant. Interpretation seeks to clarify the meaning of a verse or passage in order to understand why the Holy Spirit included the portion in Scripture. Interpretation answers the question, "What does it mean?"

The Bible is the literal Word of God and means what it says. However, there is often more than one definition of a word. For this reason, correct interpretation depends on determining the definition the writer had in mind. A dictionary is one of the best references for Bible study.

Correlation relates the verse or passage under consideration to other portions of Scripture. This prevents meanings from being forced on a passage which are not intended by the writer. Since the Bible is truth and all truth is unified, all interpretations must be consistent and coherent with the rest of the Bible.

Application is putting God's Word into practice – recognizing the voice of the Lord and responding accordingly. "When I think of Thy ways, I turn my feet to Thy testimonies; I hasten and do not delay to keep Thy commandments" (Psalm 119:59,60).

The benefit of Bible study is not derived from the method, the technique or diligent efforts to understand the text. The benefit results from obeying the voice of the Lord, receiving what He says and putting it into practice. Application does not happen by osmosis or chance – application is by obedient intent. The application may include remembering an impressive truth, changing a wrong attitude or taking a positive action.

Leading a discussion will involve taking others through these steps and drawing from their discoveries and conclusions. There are basically four types of questions in a group discussion:

20

1. *Observation Questions.* The purpose of the observation question is to reveal "What does the passage say?" Each section of an outline will need a good, thought-provoking question designed to launch the group into a meaningful discussion. An observation question will get you to the heart of the issue at hand and reveal the basic content of the section. For this reason, the observation questions should be prepared in detail in advance.

2. *Interpretation Questions.* The purpose of the interpretation question is to reveal "What does this verse mean?" The observation question will seldom be sufficient to produce the desired discussion on each section. It is difficult to fully prepare many interpretation questions because each discussion will determine its own course. However, it is helpful to have a few ideas in mind prior to the discussion.

3. *Correlation Questions.* The purpose of the correlation question is to relate different verses or passages – "How do these verses relate to each other?" If you know in advance where you want to go with the discussion, you can write your correlation questions in advance.

4. *Application Questions.* The purpose of the application question is to help each individual determine what God wants him to do as a result of the study – "What does God want you to do about this?" These questions draw out specific acts or attitudes which the passage being studied implies or commands. No study is complete without bringing attention to what should be done as a result of what was studied. These questions will be asked at the end of each section – they should *not* be saved until the end of the discussion time. Application should be emphasized throughout the discussion.

Each member of the group will have gained satisfaction investigating the Scriptures during this preparation time. Be sure to emphasize their personal preparation. Spoon-feeding those who have tasted the Word themselves is unnecessary.

Failure to ask questions, to listen to answers, or to help the group understand the content of their study may cool their desire to learn more from the Scriptures. As you allow them to dig into the Word for themselves and share their discoveries with others, they will become excited and desire to continue.

Developing Questions

There are three criteria for good questions:

- Good questions are clear.
- Good questions are relevant.
- Good questions stimulate discussion.

These criteria will help you formulate and evaluate your questions. Once you have prepared some questions, anticipate how people in your study will respond. Then revise your questions if necessary.

Before preparing your questions, consult your outline. You will prepare four questions for each major section in your outline – one observation question, one interpretation question, one correlation question and one application question.

Observation Questions

Observation questions should be carefully selected because they initiate meaningful discussion on a topic. The purpose of an observation question is to discover what the Bible says. It will determine to a large extent both the topic you will discuss and the response you will receive. Since you are trying to stimulate discussion, ask general questions which have several possible answers. For example, don't ask "What did God create?" This limits the response of the group. If you ask, "What did you learn about creation this week?", the response can include a variety of personal observations.

Observation questions must be simple and short. Avoid using "and" or "but." These usually introduce a second question. Be sure that your question can be answered by the facts contained in the study.

One way of forming comprehensive observation questions is to look at the chapter subtitle and turn it into a question. Here are some examples from the chapter "God Cares for You":

"What are some specific things God knows about you?" (from "God Knows You")

"What did you learn about God's love for you in this section?" (from "God Loves You")

"How does a person become a member of God's family?" (from "God Made You a Member of His Family")

To evaluate your observation questions, review the criteria of a good observation question.

Clarity

Does it ask for observations and facts rather than opinions and feelings?

Can it be easily remembered and understood?

Does it avoid complicated wording?

Relevance

Can it be answered from two or three of the truths in the section?

What is the underlying purpose of the question?

Does it focus attention on the main point?

Response

Will it stimulate good participation and discussion?

Does it give more than one person an opportunity to respond?

Does it draw from their personal preparation?

Interpretation Questions

Interpretation questions open up, deepen, illustrate or clarify the discussion started by the observation questions. This type of question encourages the group members to go beyond their initial observations.

Your goal is to help the group understand more fully the *meaning* of the truths discovered. Ask yourself what words and phrases may not be clearly understood and develop clarifying questions.

Often during the discussion someone will ask "What does it mean?" This *may* replace the interpretation question you have prepared. Answering the group's question is to your advantage because you are then discussing their concerns. However, do not allow the discussion to go off on a tangent.

Here are some sample interpretation questions from the lesson "God Cares for You":

"What is meant by the word 'glory' that appears in Revelation 4:11?"

"What does it mean that God 'knew' David?"

"What does unconditional love mean?"

"What does it mean that God is a Father?"

To evaluate your interpretation questions, review these criteria:

Clarity

Does the question ask "What does it mean?"

Does it help clarify the meaning?

Does it raise unnecessary problems or tangents?

Relevance

Does the question relate to truth already discovered?

Are the questions in order of importance?

Will the answers reveal what the Author of Scripture meant?

Response

Does the question lead to personal involvement by group members?

Do they have the personal knowledge to answer it?

Are the questions aimed at their personal understanding?

Correlation Questions

Good correlation questions help identify the relationship between particular truths. The purpose is to ask how the verses studied relate to each other. They should help draw individual ideas into an integrated whole.

Some examples of correlation questions from the chapter "God Cares for You" are:

"How does the fact that God created you relate to His care for you?"

"How does God's knowledge of you relate to His creating you?"

"From this study, how do you know that God loves you?"

"How does the fact that God made you part of His family relate to His care for you?"

To evaluate correlation questions, review these criteria:

Clarity

Does it ask, "How does this passage relate to other passages?"

Can the group members understand what response you want?

Relevance

Does it relate to the truths already discovered?

Does it clarify the relationship of the truths studied?

Response

Does it leave room for individual creative expression?

Can they answer the question without special knowledge of outside material?

Does it encourage people to draw from their knowledge of the Bible?

Application Questions

Application is the ultimate goal in Bible study. Correct applications depend upon accurate observation, interpretation and correlation. Application questions stimulate action and seek to utilize truths which have been discovered.

Use discretion in asking an individual a personal question in a group situation. Only ask an individual directly about his personal application when it would benefit the group present.

O.K. GUYS — HOW CAN WE APPLY THIS TRUTH TO OUR LIVES?

One way to encourage sharing is to have everyone write out an application. Then they can share the *results* of their written applications the following week. This pattern encourages writing short-range applications and expecting God to help them apply what He brought to their personal attention.

Application questions are hard to formulate, but they are the link between Bible study and daily living. You need to live with the passage, asking God to help you see where it applies. *When possible, make your application questions similar to the application questions in the prepared lesson.*

Here are some examples of application questions:

"What can you do to better glorify God as part of His creation?"

"How can you benefit from God's complete knowledge of you?"

"How do you receive this love from God?"

"What assurance do you have that you are part of God's family?

25

To evaluate application questions, review these criteria:

Clarity

Does it ask "What should I do about the truth of the passage?"

Is it clear what kind of response is expected?

Does it give freedom to choose what to do?

Purpose

Does it call for a possible and practical response?

Does it relate to truths already discovered?

Is it built on a clear understanding of the passage?

Response

Does it personally involve the group members?

Is it embarrassing to any of the group members?

Preparing a Lesson Plan

A lesson plan is a written statement of what you want to accomplish and a description of how you intend to accomplish it. It will help you organize the material to be used in the discussion. A well-prepared lesson plan is to the discussion group leader what an up-to-date map is to the traveler.

A lesson plan will help you progress confidently through a discussion because you will have a visual reminder of all the information you need at your finger tips. It will also help you stay on the topic because you can evaluate whether or not issues are tangent. Thus, you can use your time wisely.

The steps to planning are:

1. Record the subject or chapter title from the study.
2. Determine and record an outline from your study.
3. Determine and record the objectives for the lesson.

"God Cares for You"   <u>Design for Discipleship</u> <u>Book 1, Chapter 1</u>
Objective: For each of the discussion group members to acknowledge God's love by some expression of assurance of salvation.

4. Develop and record your observation, interpretation, correlation and application questions.

I. <u>God Created You</u>
   O - What did you learn in this section about God's creation?
   I - What is meant by the word 'glory' that appears in Rev. 4:11?
   C - How does the fact that God created you relate to His care for you?
   a - What can you do to better glorify God as part of His creation?

5. Plan an introduction that orients the group to the subject. In the *Design for Discipleship* series, each chapter begins with good introductory material.

> *Introduction: Review names of persons in group. Read introduction to the lesson. Pray before starting.*

6. Plan how you will conclude the study. Your conclusion ought to include a brief review and the assignment for the next meeting.

> *Conclusion: Summarize by reading the written summary at the end of the chapter. Pray specifically over your applications. Give the next assignment.*

7. Budget your time. Plan to spend two to five minutes on the introduction and conclusion. Divide the time that is left into equal parts – one for each section.

60-minute plan		90-minute plan	
Introduction -	2 minutes	Introduction -	5 minutes
Section I	- 14 minutes	Section I	- 20 minutes
Section II	- 14 minutes	Section II	- 20 minutes
Section III	- 14 minutes	Section III	- 20 minutes
Section IV	- 14 minutes	Section IV	- 20 minutes
Conclusion -	2 minutes	Conclusion -	5 minutes

"God Cares for You"

Objective: For each of the discussion group members to acknowledge God's love by some expression of assurance of salvation.

Introduction: Review names of persons in group. Read introduction to the lesson. Pray before starting.

I. God Created You

O - What did you learn in this section about God's creation?

I - What is meant by the word 'glory' that appears in Rev. 4:11?

C - How does the fact that God created you relate to His care for you?

A - What can you do to better glorify God as part of His creation?

II. God Knows You

O - What did you find out about God's knowledge of David?

I - What does it mean that God _knew_ David?

C - How does God's knowledge of you relate to His creating you?

A - How can you benefit from God's complete knowledge of you?

III. _God Loves You_
    O – What did you learn about God's love for you in this section?
    I – What does unconditional love mean?
    C – From this study, how do you know that God loves you?
    A – How do you receive this love from God?

IV. _God Made You Part of His Family_
    O – How does your study this week bring out the idea of the family?
    I – What does it mean that God is a Father?
    C – How does the fact that God made you part of His family relate to His care for you?
    A – What assurance do you have that you are part of God's family?

Conclusion: Summarize by reading the written summary at the end of the chapter.

    Pray specifically over your applications.

    Give the next assignment.

"The Person of Jesus Christ"

Objective: For each of the group members
to appreciate the two natures of
Christ and express the fact that
Christ can empathize with him.

Introduction: Review contents of
lesson from last week.
　　　Commend those who have completed
the study.
　　　Allow some to share their
completed applications.
　　　Pray before starting.

I. His Divinity
　　　O - What evidence do you see
　　　　from this section that Jesus
　　　　was God?
　　　I - Why did Christ have to be
　　　　an exact representation of
　　　　God?
　　　C - How do the prophecies about
　　　　Christ relate to His divinity?
　　　A - What reasons do you have
　　　　for believing in Christ's divinity?

II. His Humanity
　　　O - What human characteristics
　　　　did Christ exhibit?

I - Why is it important for Christ to have become human?

C - Why is it important for Christ to have been both human and divine?

A - How does the fact Jesus was human help you when you are tempted?

Conclusion: Summarize by having a group member read the summary at the end of the chapter.

Pray, thanking God specifically for things discussed.

Give the next assignment.

"The Work of Christ"

Objective: For each of the discussion
group members to understand the
life, death and resurrection of Christ
as it relates to him today and to
express at least two differences these
facts make in his life.

Introduction: Review the topics of the
chapter with the books closed.
   Read opening paragraph.
   Pray.

I. His Life
   O - How was Jesus' life like that
      of other men?
   I - What is the significance of
      His life?
   C - How does His life help fulfill
      the purpose of His coming?
   A - In what areas can you
      develop as Jesus did?

II. His Death
   O - Describe the events surrounding
      the death of Christ.
   I - Why did Christ have to die?
   C - How does Christ's death relate
      to Matthew 1:21?

A – What can you do to make yourself more acceptable to God?

III. His Resurrection

C – What evidence is there to support the resurrection of Christ?

I – Why is it important that Christ rose from the dead?

C – What is the relationship of Christ's resurrection to His work?

A – What difference does it make in your life that Christ rose from the dead?

Conclusion: Summarize by having a group member review the discussion
Pray specifically over the differences the resurrection makes in each person's life.
Give the next assignment.

34

"The Spirit Within You"

Objective: For each of the discussion group members to understand the role and influence of the Holy Spirit in his life by recognizing and expressing whether or not he is under the Spirit's control.

Introduction: Review last week's discussion.

Read the introductory paragraphs.

Pray, asking God to specifically teach each one of you during this time.

I. Christ's Ascension
   O - What events surrounded Christ's ascension?
   S - Why did Christ ascend?
   C - What is the relationship between Christ's ascension and the Second Coming?
   A - What personal hope does Christ's ascension give you?

II. His Work of Intercession
   O - How is Christ interceding for us?
   S - Why is Christ's intercession important?

C - How does His intercession relate to His ascension?

A - How can you follow Christ's example by interceding for others?

III. The Indwelling Holy Spirit

O - What is the relationship of the Holy Spirit to the believer?

I - Why did God send the Holy Spirit?

C - What is the relationship of the Holy Spirit to the ascension?

A - What evidence do you have that the Holy Spirit is in you?

IV. Living Under the Holy Spirit's Control

O - What did you learn about living under the Holy Spirit's control?

I - What can hinder you from living under His control?

C - What is the difference between being controlled by the Holy Spirit and being indwelt by the Holy Spirit?

A - How can you more fully live under the control of the Holy Spirit?

Conclusion: Summarize by having someone review the lesson

Pray specifically regarding experiencing the Holy Spirit's control.

Give the next assignment.

Leading the Discussion

Finally, after all your preparation you are ready to lead your first Bible discussion. Remember that as the leader you do not have to be a walking biblical encyclopedia with all the answers. Leading means guiding the group in such a way that each member, including yourself, amplifies and clarifies the personal insights gained through personal study as he shares. Giving the group time to talk and get acquainted will help create an environment where each member can freely share his discoveries, questions, comments and feelings.

Your lesson plan will serve as a guide for the discussion. Don't worry, however, if when the group gets together, your lesson plan does not cover all that is discussed or if you are unable to follow it exactly. Use it as a guide. Be sure to review your lesson plan, especially the objective and chapter outline, before the group gets together.

When the group settles down, check to make sure that everyone has his book, a Bible and a pen or pencil to take notes. If not, try to supply what is needed.

Begin your study by having someone read the introduction to the lesson. Most question-and-answer Bible studies have a paragraph or two which introduce the subject. Reading this passage aloud will draw everyone into the topic. For example, in the chapter "God Cares for You," someone would read the section about being a special person at the beginning of the lesson.

Once the subject has been introduced, stop and pray. The prayer will vary, but the purpose is to thank God for the time together and center on what God can teach you through the discussion. Ask God for guidance. Because you have already prepared the lesson and read the introductory paragraphs, you can ask Him to teach you specifically about the subject you will be discussing. In the chapter "God Cares for You" you might thank Him for His love and pray that as a result of this discussion each member of the group will have an increased understanding of God's love.

To insure that the discussion adequately covers the entire chapter, it will be necessary to maintain the time limits you have set for each section. Sometimes the discussion of a particularly interesting point lasts longer than you intended. Then you will need to shorten or perhaps even omit the next section.

Using Your Questions

The four types of questions – observation, interpretation, correlation and application – should be used in this order. This will take the discussion through a natural process that leads to the application of God's Word.

Start the discussion of the first section by asking your observation question. In the first section of "God Cares for You" you would ask "What did you learn in this section about God's creation?" If no one responds immediately, wait a moment or two and ask if the question was clear. If it is not clear, restate it. Look expectantly to your group for answers. After one person has made an observation, look around for others to contribute. You might ask "What else did you notice?" or "What did the rest of you discover?"

After several observations have been made, use your interpretation question. Frequently the interpretation question relates to an observation someone has made and can be introduced at that time. A good example would be, "What is meant by the word 'glory' that appears in Revelation 4:11?" Many times someone in the group will raise a question of their own. Questions from the group are desirable and should be incorporated into the discussion as long as it is not an irrelevant or digressional issue. If it does lead the discussion significantly away from the main topic, you will probably want to ask that the matter be tabled until after the chapter has been covered. If it is a good question, simply discuss it instead of your own interpretation question.

Now move to the correlation question, again looking for several people to contribute their thoughts. For example, you might ask "How does the fact that God created you relate to the fact He cares about you?"

Finally you will want to use your application question. You could ask "What can you do to glorify God as a part of His creation?"

During each section of the chapter you will want to follow the same pattern of observation, interpretation, correlation and application questions. Be sure to watch your time. If your time runs out and you need to skip a question or two, it is best to skip the interpretation or correlation questions. It's usually best to start with the observation questions and always try to include the application questions. This format is not intended to restrict you as a discussion group leader but to give you a plan which you can always refer to. With this plan in mind, you will have the freedom to let the discussion move spontaneously in new directions, knowing how and when to move it back to the main subjects of the chapter.

Discussion Techniques

The discussion can be kept moving by short, guiding questions like "What else did you notice?" or "What did you discover?" These questions could be more specifically referred to as extending, clarifying, justifying or redirecting questions. Using them can help you involve other people or draw out additional information from the group. Here are some examples:

Extending: "What else can you add to that?"
"Could you explain that more fully?"

Clarifying: "What do you mean by that?"
"Could you rephrase that statement?"

Justifying: "Would you explain that?"
"What reason can you give for that?"

Redirecting: "Mary, what do you think?"
"What did you notice, John?"

Conclusion

Draw the discussion to a close by summarizing the chapter. List the main points of the study and show how they relate. In the *Design for Discipleship* series, each chapter contains a summary which can be read.

Close in prayer either as a group or as individuals. Thank God for the time and the truths revealed during the study and discussion. Be specific. Ask him for wisdom and understanding in applying what has been discovered.

In giving the next week's assignment, state the topic or title of the next chapter. Along with the assignment, create an air of expectancy by asking a motivating question such as "If this God who loves us were to reveal Himself to us, what would He be like?" or "Why was it important for Christ to come in the form of a man?" This technique causes the group to have a questioning attitude while completing the assignment and creates a natural introduction for the next discussion.

When you review your discussion group time, you will notice many things have taken place. Group tension and conflict may have arisen from the personal interaction of members. Some of the members were very talkative, some were very quiet. Problems within the group may also have become apparent. They are normal in the life of a discussion group. In fact, they are indications of a living and maturing group! Maintaining control of the group in these situations in one of your functions as a leader.

As you prepare for and lead discussion groups over a period of time, you will become more confident in your developing style of leadership. You will learn how to ask questions and guide the discussion more effectively, how to respond appropriately to group members in various situations and how to grow in the qualities of effective group leadership.

Leading a Bible discussion group is a privilege given to you by God. Be sure to thank Him for the opportunity to guide people as they discover the truths of God's Word and trust Him to help you become increasingly effective as a discussion leader.

Improving Your Technique

Evaluating the Discussion

Too often because leaders neglect to take inventory of their experiences, they miss opportunities for improvement. Below are some questions which will help you evaluate the behavior of the group and your ability to lead.

Your leading techniques:

Did you lead or were you led?

Did you listen?

Were you sensitive to group members' needs?

Were there any tangents? How did they occur? How could they have been avoided or best answered?

Biblical context:

Was the information carefully observed, interpreted, correlated and applied?

Did you keep to the subject? Was the material covered? If not, why not?

Planning and preparation:

Did you follow the plan closely? Why or why not?

Did you consider yourself to have prepared adequately? If not, what was needed?

What did you learn that you could include in future planning?

Participation of group:

Did everyone you expected come to the group discussion? If not, why not?

Was each person stimulated to contribute his best? If not, what could you have done to accomplish this?

Did anyone ever question the group, or a group member question another group member? Who?

Application of the truth:

Were the applications in keeping with the content of the study?

Were the applications shared specific and practical?

Were the applications from the previous discussion carried out?

Personal relationships within the group:

How well do the members know each other?

How well do the members listen to each other?

These questions will stimulate further thinking in your own mind as to what is expected of you as a group leader. Continue to ask the Lord for wisdom and diligence in leading the flock of people that he has put under your care.

"Shepherd the flock of God among you, not under compulsion, but voluntarily, according to the will of God; and not for sordid gain, but with eagerness; nor yet as lording it over those allotted to your charge, but proving to be examples to the flock."

I Peter 5:2,3 (NASB)

In the process of developing skill in a method or technique, there is a tendency to fall into one or more of the following three traps:

1. *Comparing yourself with others.* The Word warns us against doing this in II Corinthians 10:12, "Not that we venture to class or compare ourselves with some of those who commend themselves. But when they measure themselves by one another, and compare themselves with one another, they are without understanding." Comparison is a denial of God's special place for you. Each individual is unique and the Lord has given every person special abilities that need to be developed.

2. *Discouragement.* When the discussion does not meet your expectations, you may have a tendency to become discouraged – to focus on what went wrong. Recognizing obstacles and mistakes will alert you to new ways of improving your ability to lead the discussion. This is part of the learning process. Don't allow Satan to discourage you; remember that God is honored when His Word goes forth. God is a God of encouragement. You can always trace discouragement to Satan. So don't get discouraged.

3. *Giving up.* Don't throw in the towel. There is a need to stick with a goal until completion . . "Better is the end of a thing than its beginning . . . " (Ecclesiastes 7:8). This is especially true when you know for certain it is the will of God. Everyone has to start where they are and move in the direction of progress. "Never give up" is the best policy to follow in learning how to lead discussion groups. In due time, you will prosper.

44

Often when evaluating, the leader is aware only of the negative – the mistakes, the problems and the omissions. Remember that an important function of evaluation is to be aware of the positive – What went right? What was good in this discussion? Maintaining the strong points of your leading is as important as improving the weak areas. The most exciting outcome of your discussion group is not the development of your ability to lead – it is that God's Word is being studied, discussed and applied. God is using each discussion you lead to proclaim His Word.

Improving Your Leadership

In order to be an effective Bible discussion group leader you should:

Know well the passage to be studied.

It will take extra time to dig a little deeper and to look at the verses to be studied, but there is no substitute for diligent preparation and prayer. Do not be sidetracked from the priority of intensive personal study. When you stop studying, you can no longer lead your discussion group as effectively as possible.

Be excited about the discoveries of group members.

Often a Bible discussion leader will get excited only about what he himself has discovered from the text of Scripture. He acknowledges what others find with a nod of the head, an appreciating remark or a further question, but he fails to get excited about the new truths that group members are discovering. Because you have previously discovered a truth that someone is just now discovering, do not quench his quest for new truth by your superior attitude! Get excited about what others discover – and show it.

Utilize your sense of humor.

Spontaneity and freedom are important areas to be developed in the life of any leader. Humor that is well-placed and well-timed, appropriate to the audience and to the context of what is being studied, will help create a favorable environment for the discussion. The leader must develop his own style of humor and not try to merely imitate another's style.

Be enthusiastic.

A leader is not necessarily the one who comes up with the best observations, interpretations, correlations and applications. Neither is he the one who uncovers the most revealing background material, character sketches or trivial facts. The leader should, however, be the one with the most enthusiasm. Make your discussion one they will never forget! Ask God to give you a spirit of enthusiasm as you prepare for the discussion and as you lead it. Your attitude will help determine the attitude of each member in your group.

Use memorable and relevant illustrations and visualizations.

Eye-catchers and ear-catchers captivate human interest. Simple illustrations communicate more readily than the complex. A picture, a drawing, a story ... personal illustrations can provide your group members with a point of identification with you. Encourage the participants in the group to share their illustrations and visual aids.

Using Questions More Effectively

Asking questions to help a person discover scriptural principles for himself is not a new technique. Jesus used over 100 questions in the Gospel.

There were many purposes behind the questions of Jesus. One man has said Jesus " ... came not to answer questions, but to ask them; not to settle men's souls, but to provoke them."

Some of the purposes of Jesus' questions were:

- To secure information (Luke 8:30)
- To express emotion (John 3:10)
- To recall the known (Mark 2:25,26)
- To awaken conscience (Matthew 23:17)
- To elicit faith (Mark 8:29)
- To create a dilemma (Mark 3:4)

Jesus often used the leading type of question which suggested the answer He wanted but which allowed the one questioned to draw his own conclusion. The nature of the leading question is to lead toward a conclusion while not forcing acceptance of the answer.

For example, in Matthew 5:13 Jesus asked this question in the Sermon on the Mount, "You are the salt of the earth; but if salt has lost its taste, how shall its saltiness be restored?" The conclusion is obvious. You need to stay salty to have the effect of salt.

Sometimes He used questions to stop the opposition. He asked questions that His foes were unwilling to answer. Compare Matthew 21:25-27, Matthew 22:45 and Luke 14:5,6.

From Jesus' example you can see that your job as a discussion group leader is to help others discover truth for themselves. Don't tell them something they could conclude for themselves if you were to ask them the right questions. Never tell when you can ask. Stop and think of a good question which will allow the group to draw their own conclusions.

Another thing to notice from Jesus' example is the tone in which He asked questions. To Him, *how* He asked was as important as *what* He asked. The following hints will help you in asking questions.

✳ **Avoid using close-ended questions.**

A close-ended question leaves no room for continuing the conversation because it usually requires a "yes" or "no" answer. An open-ended question requires opinions or further thinking.

Close-ended:
   "Did Jesus die on the Cross to save us?"
   "Do you think that Jesus should be the Lord of your life?"
Open-ended:
   "Why do you think Jesus died on the Cross?"
   "Why do you feel Jesus should be Lord of your life?"

Sometimes starting a question with a helping word creates a close-ended question (can, do, should, etc.). Starting a question with why, what or how usually creates an open-ended question.

Close-ended:
   "Can this be accomplished?"
Open-ended:
   "How can this be accomplished?"

Be prepared to wait for an answer.

Waiting demonstrates your real interest and concern. Give a person time to think. You may want to restate the question. Also be attentive to second thoughts. Often a person will think of more to say on an issue or be able to clarify his position after he makes his first statement. It is common for people to think of what they should have said. If you sense this, be alert enough to come back for more information.

   "Do you have any more thoughts on that?"
   "Would you like to add anything else?"

Listen attentively.

Use your eyes to look at the person – don't glance off because he doesn't seem eager to respond. Be observant of what people say and use their statements to formulate other questions. It was said that "President Kennedy made you think he had nothing else to do except ask you questions and listen, with extraordinary concentration, to your answer. You knew that for the time being he had blotted out both the past and the future."

✳ **Use questions that deal with feelings as well as facts.**

Facts will tell you what a person knows. His feelings will tell you how he really feels about it. Memorization of facts alone is no guarantee that the principles involved are understood.

Fact questions:
   "What are the two things he stressed?"

"What was the main point he covered?"
"What are the steps in leading a person to Christ?"

Feeling questions:
"Why did he stress those two things?"
"How do you use these steps in leading a person to Christ?"
"How did you react to his main point?"

Convictions are formed internally as people learn to express verbally how they feel about certain issues. Some key words to use are feel, think, mean, respond, react.

"What do you think about that?"
"How do you react to that?"

Sometimes you can use a combination of fact and feeling questions.

"What is his greatest strength?"
"Why do you feel that is true?"

✳ Deal with people's true interests.

Questions that come the closest to people's true interests get the best answers. Learn how to identify a person's frame of reference. Find out not only *what* he wants to talk about, but *how* he wants to talk about it. Take something from their answers to formulate your next question. Let them talk and use their words. These words indicate their interests and people appreciate hearing their own thoughts being used.

Answer questions with questions.

Often people will ask a question when their real desire is to tell you what they think. "Don't you think that ... ?" and "Do you think that ... ?" are examples of this. A good way to avoid a premature answer is to ask "What do you think?" This is what they really want – an opportunity to express their views.

50

Sometimes people will try to force you to defend yourself. Their purpose is to show you that they disagree and to get you to take a position so they can attack you. They sometimes start with a question like "Do you think the Bible is inspired?" You can respond with "What do you think?" Then they can express themselves and you haven't had to declare a position yet.

✴ Learn when and how to use direct and indirect questions.

A direct question causes a person to take an open stand and declare a position. An indirect question is sometimes in the third person and objective. You should be careful not to use direct questions too soon in your relationships with people or they may become offended. Be sure you have their confidence first.

Direct:
"What do you think, Bill?"
"Are you a Christian?"
"Is Jesus the Lord of your life?"

These are personal questions directed at getting to the point. These cut down your effectiveness if you use them too quickly and too often.

Indirect:
"What does the Bible say about this?"
"What is a real Christian?"
"How can you tell that Jesus is Lord of someone's life?"

These are impersonal questions directed at anyone. They are good questions to use in witnessing and in leading Bible discussions.

Avoid questions that assume an answer.

Don't oversuggest answers in your questions. Lead people and direct them toward the answers, but don't drag them into the answers. Rhetorical questions fall into this category and don't even need expressed answers. They are obvious.

Poor:
"Jesus died on the Cross for you, didn't He?"
"The purpose of evangelism is to reach the unsaved, isn't it?"

Good:
"What do you feel was the primary purpose of Christ's death?"
"What do you think the purpose of evangelism is?"

✴ Use questions that focus on a specific item.

Use words or phrases that cause one's mind to crystallize or focus on only one or just a few key ideas. Use such words as "key thing," "main point," "most important" or "primary emphasis."

Poor:

> "How did your discussion go?"

Good:

> "What was the most interesting thing that happened in your discussion group?"

The real key in asking questions is your genuine concern and interest in people. Genuine questioning conveys the attitude that you truly are interested in what people have to say. You cannot conceal a lack of concern. True dialogue begins where people genuinely want to share in another person's thoughts. If you are really interested in what the other person feels and thinks, you will never be ineffective in asking questions.

Aids to Creativity

Using a variety of approaches in leading your group will add zest to the discussion. Creative presentations of scriptural truths enhance learning by capturing interest and stimulating discussion. Employing audio-visual aids is one way to be a creative leader. The ability to learn and retain knowledge is increased when audio-visual aids are used.

How do you discover ways to present ideas creatively? Many familiar objects become teaching tools when used properly. You can make other tools, too. Here are some examples of how to use everyday objects creatively to illustrate a point:

- *A map of Bible lands* will help the group visualize Paul's journey as they study the Book of Acts.
- *A horse's bridle* will help illustrate principles from James 3 if you place it in front of the group and ask them how it relates to the control of the tongue.
- *A model or picture of the human body* will stimulate discussion on the role of the church as Christ's Body.
- *Newspaper cartoons* will often illustrate a biblical principle and add a bit of humor at the same time.
- *A drop of dye in a jar of water* can be used to illustrate the spread of the Gospel throughout the world.

The Bible uses a multitude of picture words. People are likened to salt, lamps, sheep, warriors, etc. Jesus is referred to as a door, a light, a shepherd and bread. Thus, you can easily use any of these objects and pictures to add vitality to your discussion.

You can also use charts, posters, puppets, models or slides. Many Christian organizations and churches produce taped messages which can be used in a discussion.

Sources for ideas include your local library, church media department or bookstore. You can also write publishers and producers for listings of visual aids. Ask for catalogues, listings of films, filmstrips, slides, pictures, overhead transparencies, etc. You can also ask schoolteachers and friends for ideas. Teachers often have imaginative ideas about how to communicate knowledge.

When developing and using teaching aids, be sure to keep them simple and clear. They should only include the essentials and be pertinent. Be sure they are suitable for the group which will see them.

Teaching aids can be used at any point in the discussion, but often you will want to include an aid in the introduction and/or conclusion of your discussion. These are very important items in the discussion and an audio-visual aid can captivate interest and place emphasis on particular truths. However, it is better to use two or three meaningful aids than to fill the discussion with a number of irrelevant ones.

Introducing Conversational Prayer

...AND ALSO LORD PLEASE BLESS ALL THE NICE MISSIONARIES IN KENYA, UGANDA, ETHIOPIA, LITHUANIA, GUATEMALA, BRAZIL, INDONESIA, TAIWAN, KOREA, BORA BORA...

Praying together is vital for an effective discussion group. After people have discussed what they have discovered in the Bible and how they have applied the Word to their lives, a time of praise, petition and thanksgiving is appropriate. Conversational prayer is a simple method of prayer which helps group members learn how to pray together. Individuals learn to pray as an interrelated group. Each person should say what they think or feel with honesty and openness before the Lord and one another.

As the leader, you will want to begin to pray by sharing your concerns with the Lord. Use "I," "me" and "my" instead of "we," "us" or "they." You will want to keep your prayer to a maximum of one or two sentences so that you do not monopolize the conversation — you will also be setting the example for the next person. Let the group members pray voluntarily. Do not force them to pray by going around the circle.

This conversational pattern may continue back and forth in the group until a subject has been covered. Then the conversational dialogue should move on to another topic.

People who have never been able to pray out loud before others will soon be able to enter the conversation quite freely. This type of prayer is completely spontaneous without the traditional language or archaic form. At first a group member may only be able to utter an "amen" or "me too, Lord," but before long he will enjoy entering into the group prayer experience with enthusiasm.

Keep in mind these simple guidelines for conversational prayer:

- Pray *briefly* so everyone has the opportunity to pray several times.
- Pray *audibly* so that everyone can hear what is being prayed.
- Pray *topically* so that everyone has the opportunity to pray about the same subject.
- Pray *specifically* so that everyone can focus on a particular request.

Be sure to note and thank God for His answers to your group prayer. The group will be encouraged as they see specific answers to specific prayer requests.

"Again I say to you, if two of you agree on earth about anything they ask, it will be done for them by My Father in heaven. For where two or three are gathered in My name, there am I in the midst of them" (Matthew 18:19,20).

New Approaches to Discussion

In order to keep your Bible study from becoming dull, you will want to continually try new approaches to your discussion. Remember, however, all true creativity is built on fundamental principles. In leading a Bible discussion you can use a wide variety of techniques in discussing the subject, but be sure to build around the observation, interpretation, correlation and application questions.

Dr. Howard Hendricks, professor of Christian education at Dallas Theological Seminary, lists ten different types of group interaction that can be utilized and adopted for group meetings. Use these as takeoff points for developing your own techniques.

Discussion

Definition. A co-operative search for the solution to a problem. It often is merely small talk with no plan or purpose. It can be creative interaction where problems are solved, decisions are made and learning takes place.

Details. Discussion is valid when information is needed *from* the group; when decisions must be made *by* the group; when tension and unrest exist *within* the group; and when information has been given *to* the group. The leader starts, guides, stimulates, moderates and summarizes. Discussion has well been called "the art of thinking independently together." It allows for expression, interaction, analysis and synthesis. Ideas are discovered. Ignorance and prejudice are discouraged — for a mind cannot remain completely closed when its contents are shared!

info from group = good
by group = bad

Buzz Groups

Definition. Small, informal groups designed for a minimum of organization and a maximum of participation.

Details. The group is divided into smaller groups of two to six members each. Each buzz group appoints a leader and a secretary. A subject is assigned and the small groups discuss it for a designated time. After this they convene and share their ideas and conclusions. Buzz groups should work for short periods of time usually six to eight minutes. Topics must be specific. This method facilitates interaction among all members and it stimulates analysis and solution of problems. "Men are never so likely to settle a question rightly as when they discuss it freely."

Brainstorming

Definition. A procedure designed to obtain a quantity of ideas.

Details. The group is given a problem. Each member is asked to direct his attention to the problem and to contribute any idea that comes to his mind. Since criticism tends to stifle creativity; evaluation and judgment of ideas is withheld for the present. The group is challenged to think of as many ideas as they can and given a specified time length to do it. The ideas are recorded and evaluated later. During the brainstorming session judgment is suspended, because judgment jams imagination. Mental "freewheeling" is encouraged because quantity breeds quality. "Hitchhiking" is utilized to turn good ideas into better ideas. Brainstorming is essentially "creative collaboration." It can be an individual as well as a group effort.

Circle Response

The process of obtaining the opinions and ideas of each individual member of the group. This is accomplished by beginning with any one person, and continuing around the group, asking each one to express himself in regard to the given subject.

Debate

Definition. The presentation, defense and refutation of opposing issues.

Details. Discussion seeks new insights; debate seeks to prove a point. Debate is formal; when informal it is an argument. Presentations are given by the affirmative and then the negative. This is followed by rebuttals by the negative and then the affirmative. The entire proceedings are under the leadership of a moderator.

Role Playing

Definition. Spontaneously playing the part of a particular person in a particular set of circumstances.

Details. A problem is raised. The scene is set to portray the problem. The roles are defined and members of the group chosen to play these roles. The role players are prepared to act and the group is prepared to observe. The scene is enacted spontaneously and cut when the objective has been obtained. Evaluation and analysis then follow in the group discussion. The scene may be replayed if necessary. Scenes should be short; from three to six minutes. This technique enables and forces people to think from

58

various points of view. It puts a person in the "other fellow's shoes." It helps to gain insight into how people think and react, and it helps to teach people what to say and what not to say in specific circumstances.

Listen Teams

The group is divided into two or more "listening teams." These teams are then instructed to look and / or listen for certain things in the following presentation. The presentation can be through lecture, role playing, film, etc. After the presentation the teams meet separately to compare notes and to formulate their observations. Then the results are shared and discussed by the group as a whole. This method heightens attention and discernment. It challenges people to listen intelligently and creatively.

Panel

Selected representatives discuss informally the subject at hand under the guidance of a moderator. Ideas are exchanged, varying opinions are discussed and problems are solved. The audience may also participate.

Forum

Under the guidance of a moderator questions are asked by the audience and directed to the resource individuals present before the group.

Symposium

Several speakers give brief presentations to the audience. This is followed by a moderated discussion among the speakers, with the audience often allowed to ask questions and make comments.

These different types of group interaction can be utilized in the process of meeting together throughout the weeks of group Bible discussion. One important guideline to remember is always to use the *best* technique to communicate the stated objective of the discussion time. Let your objectives determine your group techniques – not the other way around. Group techniques are not to be used as gimmicks or ends in themselves, but to help people dig into the Word and interact over their conclusions. A technique is only useful if it helps communicate the content and context of your discussion group goal.

Roles
People Play

Dr. Hendricks says, "Each member of the group is faced with the right and the responsibility of being a mature participant. To accomplish this he must apply himself to the task of being an effective group member, constantly evaluating himself and his relationships with others."

In the following amusing and informative material, Dr. Hendricks describes roles people play in a group situation. You will find it helpful in evaluating the members of your group.

Characteristics of Immaturity

Onlooker	Content to be a silent spectator. Nods, smiles and frowns. Other than this he is a passenger instead of a crew member.
Monopolizer	Brother Chatty. Rambles roughshod over the rest of the conversation with his verbal dexterity. Tenaciously clings to his right to say what he thinks – sometimes without thinking.
Belittler	This is Mr. Gloom. He takes the dim view. Minimizes the contributions of others. Usually has three good reasons why "it will never work."
Wisecracker	Feels called to a ministry of humor. Mr. Cheerio spends his time and talent as the group playboy. Indifferent to the subject at hand he is always ready with the clever remark.

Manipulator	Brother Ulterior knows the correct approach to the problem, obviously. He manipulates the proceedings so his plan will be adopted.
Hitchhiker	Never had an original thought in his life. Unwilling to commit himself. Sits on the sidelines until the decision has jelled, then jumps on the bandwagon.
Pleader	Chronically afflicted with obsessions. Always pleading for some cause or certain actions. Feels led to share this burden frequently. One-track mind.
Sulker	Born in the objective case and lives in the kickative mood. The group won't accept his worthy contribution so he sulks.

Characteristics of Maturity

Proposer	Initiates ideas and action. Keeps things moving
Encourager	Brings others into the discussion. Encourages others to contribute. Emphasizes the value of their suggestions and comments. Stimulates others to greater activity by approval and recognition.
Clarifier	The one who has the facility to step in when confusion, chaos and conflict dominate. He defines the problem concisely. He points out the issues clearly.
Analyzer	Examines the issues closely. Weighs the suggestions carefully. Never accepts anything without first "thinking it through."
Explorer	Always moving into new and different areas. Probing relentlessly. Never satisfied with the obvious or the traditional.
Mediator	Facilitates agreement or harmony between members; especially those who are making phrases at each other. Seeks to find mediating solutions acceptable to all.
Synthesizer	Is able to put the pieces together. Brings the different parts of the solution or plan together and synthesizes them.
Programmer	The one who is ready with the ways and means to put the proposal into effect. Adept at organization. Moves in the realm of action.

One way to use this material is to read this section to your discussion group and then have them react and respond to the various roles in the group. You may want them to privately evaluate their role in the group and then publicly discuss it at the next meeting. This type of evaluation helps the group members see themselves for what they really are. It gives each member an appreciation for the other members in the group. The humorous way the above captions are written may help clarify the personal involvement of each member in the group.

Constructive Group Tension

In most discussions controversy, tension and excitement are avoided! Many leaders associate conflict with dissension and strife and, therefore, try to stay away from any semblance of disagreement. Some disagreements occur because of misguided questions, petty issues and false doctrine, but not all disagreement is a result of these things and not all disagreement is bad, wrong or un-Christlike. The group that sails along always agreeing with one another may be the group that is not thinking.

When disagreements arise ask yourself "Is it important?" or "Is it of interest?" Then decide if it is worth the time to discuss the controversial subject.

Some of the most profitable discussions and group interaction have taken place over an issue or question that introduced tension, disagreement and a difference of opinion. During these times the group leader can point the members to the Word as the final authority. (In every difference of opinion the final court of appeal is either reason, tradition or the Word of God.) These times of tension provide an ideal opportunity to take the group into the Word and let the Word settle the question rather than tradition or reason.

There are many ways to create a difference of opinion and to get honest answers out in the open. Having each member in turn respond to a specific question, staging a debate, or intentionally having someone take the opposite view on an issue can create the kind of disagreement that forces the group into the Word.

Sometimes questions and their converse generate a confrontation.

"Why is it necessary to memorize Scripture?"
"Why isn't it necessary to memorize Scripture?"

Sometimes questions that require a decision generate a confrontation.

"Which is better – to do what is right when you
don't feel like it, or to wait to get the right
motive, feeling or desire?"

Sometimes controversial questions generate a confrontation.
"Why does God allow suffering?"

Clarification occurs when the leader takes control and leads the group toward resolution. The goal is to get the group into the Word to discover for themselves the answer to the tension caused by the variety of opinions. Sometimes resolution occurs when the group realizes that the Word doesn't give a specific answer but allows room for several opinions. The leader should be ready with some summary questions and a summary statement which puts the conclusion of the Word into one sentence. The group can then apply the principle with its many possible applications and implications.

The type of group tension that creates animosity, division and strife is warned against in II Timothy 2:23, "Have nothing to do with stupid, senseless controversies; you know that they breed quarrels." I Timothy 1:5 says, "Whereas the aim of our charge is love that issues from a pure heart and a good conscience and sincere faith." Aim toward love! But don't avoid healthy group tension.

Turning Problems into Opportunities

In every discussion group you will run into problems. But these problems or obstacles can be turned into opportunites with proper handling. Here are some ideas.

How to control the talkative.

Calling for contributions from others often helps – "What do the rest of you think?" You can also refer these questions to a specific member of the group. In some situations you may have to take control of the discussion and call for a show of hands before anyone responds. Then you can call on the group members in turn. Sometimes it is necessary to talk privately with the "talker," explaining the necessity of group participation. You may be able to enlist him to help you draw others in. This will not only solve the problem of his dominating the discussion, it will also help him become more sensitive to other people.

How to get back on track.

A verbal recognition of the problem usually helps – "This is interesting. However, we have left our topic. Perhaps we could discuss this further after we finish our topic." Or you may present a thought-provoking question to draw the discussion back to the initial thought or topic. At times, you can suggest tabling the question or idea until after the discussion when those who want to can discuss it further. Your attitude toward the tangent is most important.

How to handle wrong answers.

Never tell a person he is wrong. You may want to direct the same question to others in the group. For example, "Okay, what do others think?" or "Has anyone some other Scripture which may help us here?" or "What does someone else have to say about this?" You may want to restate the question or ask another question which would help clarify or stimulate further thought. Always keep others from losing face or getting embarrassed because of a wrong answer.

How to handle silence.

Don't be afraid of pauses or try to fill in verbal voids. If you give people time to think, *they* will ask good questions as the discussion progresses. By being patient, you may be surprised with the number of excellent thoughts the group comes up with. These silent times may seem to be uncomfortable times, but don't be embarrassed or feel like you must say something.

How to handle difficult questions.

Don't ever be afraid of saying, "I don't know." If you do not know the answer, don't pretend to. You can always find the answer later or have someone else research it. A member of the group may have a good answer. There is no merit in being known as a "know-it-all." If you always have the answer, your discussion group will turn into a lecture.

How to cover the passage or chapter.

Make a determined effort to cover the entire portion allotted for the discussion. Continually getting bogged down in details and falling behind can have a very demoralizing effect on the group. Moving ahead gives a feeling of accomplishment and success. If you have trouble getting through the material, you may have tried to cover too much material and may need to cut back.

How to spark a lethargic group.

Generally the group will respond to the attitude of the leader. Pray for enthusiasm. If you want them to be a little enthusiastic, then you may have be to overly enthusiastic. The source of enthusiasm is a desire for the Lord Himself, for His Word, the commitment to be a disciple of Jesus. The leader, by example, will have to demonstrate these convictions. You cannot expect excitement from a group if you are not excited yourself.

How to handle controversial subjects.

To smother honest questions and convictions is stifling. A Bible discussion marked by the pleasant word, the smile, the pious utterance or the well-verbalized prayer can be an unproductive study. Even when a group is seriously looking for truth, there may be a temptation to skirt the difficult issues of life and rely on superficial answers. The best way to handle controversial topics is to see what the Word of God has to say and rest the verdict on the principles or commands of the Bible that apply to the situation. God's Word is the ultimate authority.

How to draw out applications.

Expect God to speak through His Word in such a way that people will realize that it applies to them. The Holy Spirit will bring the passage to bear upon their thinking and lives. Be direct in your approach where the Word of God is direct. You can help people see the relevance of the Word for themselves through questions of application. So learn to ask effective application questions. "What does this mean to you?" or "Is there anything that you can do about this today?" Learn how to share your own applications with honesty and humility. Openness on your part will create openness on theirs.

How to show reinforcement.

Reinforcement refers to the approval of the group's responses. You show approval of group responses through such overt behavior as acknowledging an answer with comments like "good," "that's right," a positive nod of the head, a smile or other more subtle behavior. Reinforcement may also take the form of support of an anticipated response. For example, "Take a moment to think. I know you can answer this." You may also reinforce participation even when a wrong answer has been given, "That is a thoughtful answer." Too often leaders are pleased with answers, but fail to show any outward sign of their pleasure. Overuse of one encouraging word, inappropriate exhortation or seemingly insincere enthusiasm may not serve the purpose of reinforcement.

How to increase listening ability.

Listening is the ability to really hear what others are saying. It calls for hearing not only what they say, but what they can't say and what they won't say. It requires concentration and attention aimed at the members of the group. Some members tend to think more about what they want to say rather than about what the others are saying. They become preoccupied with their own thoughts. One way to get rid of this lapse in listening is to have each person in turn summarize what has just been said by the previous person. Doing this requires the members to concentrate on every contribution to the discussion.

Training Others to Lead Out

As the discussion group leader, you should begin to sensitize yourself to the needs and desires of the group members for further ministry and service. Begin to train an assistant who can take your place or start another group.

When choosing an assistant, look for a person who will:

- Pray with you for the group on a regular basis.
- Help you lead the group more effectively by
  going over the evaluation with you after each
  discussion. Discuss what happened in each
  discussion, why it happened and how to improve.
  He will often be able to see more clearly
  what is happening in the group because he is
  not under the pressure of asking, redirecting
  and answering questions.
- Learn how to lead a group himself so that
  if you happen to be absent he can take the
  responsibility to lead it.
- Be prepared to start and lead another group.

When people become interested in joining a group after it has begun, you can do one of two things: either invite them to join an existing group in its early stages or start another group.

As the number of people in the group grows, make plans for starting another group. Six is the best number for a discussion group. Your assistant, who has been helping you and learning about leading a group, is probably the one you will ask to lead the new group.

Frequently the group will not want to divide. After all, it may be the first time that they have really gotten to know other Christians well. So you will need to share with them some of the reasons for dividing.

If the group grows too large, all the values of being a small group decrease: fellowship becomes less intimate, personal involvement diminishes, stimulation to prepare and opportunity to share lessens and the atmosphere becomes less of a group of close friends and more of a committee meeting.

On the other hand in a *small* group:

- Each member counts and knows it. He will be missed if absent.
- There will be time for each to contribute.
- Regular study will be stimulated.
- There will be better stimulation of personal application.
- Each will be more free to share.
- All can get to know the others well.
- Most homes or rooms can accommodate a small group.
- More people are willing to lead a small group than a large one and, thus, have the opportunity to grow in spiritual leadership.

Help the new leader arrange a place for the new group to meet and let all the members know of the new arrangements and when they will take place. Let the new leader exercise his responsibilities. Be available to give him advice and encouragement.

As you and your previous assistant choose assistants and train them to be leaders, you will be able to see how you have begun to start a process that will result in an ever increasing number of people becoming disciples of Jesus Christ!

MATERIALS REFERENCED

Design for Discipleship
Six books designed to teach the
essentials of Christian discipleship.

Leader's Guide for Evangelistic Bible Studies (Using the Gospel of John)
A step-by-step guide for conducting an
evangelistic Bible study. Participants
do not prepare in advance.

Advanced Search the Scriptures
An approach to chapter analysis Bible study.

These materials may be purchased from:
Customer Services
NavPress
P.O. Box 20
Colorado Springs, Colorado 80901

FREE NAVIGATOR DISCIPLESHIP MATERIALS CATALOG

A catalog containing a listing of
other materials produced by
NavPress may also
be obtained by writing to
Customer Services
NavPress
P.O. Box 20
Colorado Springs, Colorado 80001